# Racer

*For Melanie*

# Racer

*Kevin Fegan*

www.fiveleaves.co.uk
www.kevinfegan.co.uk

# **Racer**
## *Kevin Fegan*

First published in 2003 by
Five Leaves Publications,
PO Box 81, Nottingham NG5 4ER
info@fiveleaves.co.uk
www.fiveleaves.co.uk

(c) Kevin Fegan

Five Leaves acknowledges financial support
from Arts Council England

ISBN: 0 907123 44 9

Typeset by Four Sheets Design and Print
Printed in Great Britain

**RACER**

The shortest distance between
two points is a straight line.
It is a race against time for all of us
so my job is making straight lines
out of corners and, this year,
I am straighter than ever before.
Know me as *the Crow*,
not the common carrion kind
but a hooded Crow of Celtic origin,
I wear my grey and black colours with pride,
watch me fly, watch me ride.
Everyone will tell you
what a really nice guy I am;
I know they are all scared of the Crow.
I am the number one
regulator of other birds,
I keep them in their place –
behind me. I nest alone,
unmolested in tall riverside trees,
I observe and I remember,
I rob and wreck other nests where I please,
I take out other birds,
eat their eggs, their chicks,
my caw is harsh and resonant,
I perch on high and announce my presence.
my skill is there for all to see,
my crafty intelligence carries no apology,
I hide nothing.

This beautiful migration
is an early Summer sensation.
40,000 brightly
coloured, bird-like machines
descend on the island.
Shocking purples and racing greens,
blood-red heads, yellow-backs, all-blacks,
leather-backs of every description,
open-face, full-face,
snub-nosed, pointed beaks, all manner
of stripes and spots from head to feet,
red-breasts and patterned crests,
full-fairings, half-fairings, no-fairings,
some with exotic names like Ducati,
Moto Guzzi and warrior names
like Triumph and Fireblade,
noble names like Aprillia and MV Agusta
alongside the more dominant, popular
names of Yamaha and Suzuki,
Honda and Kawasaki.
Racers, trailies, customs, streetfighters,
all sweeping into the harbour
for a fortnight among their own kind.
500 of them,
from 22 different countries,
are here to compete.
The rest want a piece of the action,
to share in the excitement of speed,
to absorb the atmosphere
and there is a perverse fear in the air
because, one way or another,

everyone is here to race
in this extraordinary show
of abandon and bravado.
When it comes to risk,
it doesn't come much scarier than this.
Take an ordinary road:
lamp-posts, brick walls, buildings, kerbs,
trees, water and hills,
hump-back bridges, blind summits,
double 'S' bends — you name it,
the island has got it, over
37 miles of beautiful grey road.
Take a modern engine, bolted
onto a lightweight metal frame, one seat,
two wheels and a simple set of handlebars
and race on these roads at speeds
up to 200 m.p.h.
Let's see how good you really are?

Truth is, I've never won a TT.
I bull myself up as a champion
but I've never made it to the top
perch on the podium.
I'm 39 years old, don't know
how much longer I can go on.
So many races have come and gone
and never the champion I dreamed of,
champion of the streets, where I started,
where I come from, that's why it matters.
This time, this time I'm in with a real chance,
I was fastest in practice

so I'm first off this morning.
Every ten seconds riders are released:
they'll all start behind me,
it's up to me to keep it that way.
This is the bit I don't like:
the waiting, the butterflies.
We've made our choice of tyres:
it's wet which favours the nutters.
I like the wet, I prefer it
to the sun in my eyes,
if I can keep my bravery
this side of madness, I can turn
the occasional slides
and waivers into victory
and stay alive to ride again.
The leader boards are ready,
the white triangular clock is ticking,
I look around at the grandstand
on one side of the road
and the cemetery on the other,
preparations are underway:
the white church is being cleaned
and fresh plots are being turned.
A gang of Born Again Middle-Aged Bikers,
*Bambis*, pass innocently by the gates:
they're here in their full matching leathers
to test their Sunday dry-weather-only
riding skills with their mates
on the ultimate road race circuit.
I watch the local bobbies
in their white spiked helmets

keeping a crowd of hell's angels
with video cameras at bay.
Through a gap in the stand I can see
rows and rows of merchandising
where the long hair and the short hair,
the grey hair and the no hair,
the blond hair and the brown hair,
the red hair and the dyed hair
buy their t-shirts and cups,
baseball caps and books,
videos and magazines,
souvenir programmes and ice-creams
as the industry behind the scenes
increases year by year.
Cars have suddenly disappeared
from the face of the earth,
even a Ferari would fail to turn heads here
Two wheels fast, four wheels last.
The teams are in their pits, ready
to pitch their wits against the road conditions,
the tyres are out of their blankets
and onto the machines,
time for a little magic of my own.
Call it superstition,
I won't allow my bike to take up position
until I've done a figure of eight,
my lucky number,
no point tempting fate, is there?

The Production 600 is my
favourite race. I'm sitting astride
my Suzuki GSXR,
a bike that anyone could buy
over the counter, on a road
that anyone could ride.
Up and down the country
thousands of bikers own this type
of machine and dream of racing
it as fast as me.
Three laps, 113 miles in all,
at an average speed of
120 m.p.h.,
that's Birmingham to London
in less than one hour
via the tourist route
on winding 'A' roads,
not on a straight stretch of motorway.

The waiting is finally over
as the flag falls.
A simple twist of the wrist
results in a surge of adrenaline
as I pull away from the start line
into a 100 m.p.h. wheelie,
I hang on tight to my grips
and my knees squeeze against the petrol tank;
you see, all those urban clichés
about the machine throbbing between your legs
are true, not quite the same as getting laid
but it has all the rush

of that first sexual encounter,
whoosh and you're away,
racing through the gears
down towards Bray Hill.

In years to come, when
we invite computers
to take up residence
under our skin, when
micro robots course through
our veins at incredible speeds,
we will look back at these
early attempts at synthesis
between man and machine
with more than a little pride
and say, *How could they
achieve such a union
between engine and rider?*

Concentrate, that's the key.
When I race the TT, I feel
an overwhelming sense of cheating death,
it's like robbing a locksmiths,
the risk and the pleasure
of an immoral victory.
I feel in touch with my life,
I know I'm alive on a motorbike.
I'm fit and healthy:
my body is finely tuned to process
information quickly to my brain.
My senses are on overdrive:

I see the white markers flashing by,
I smell the damp on the road
from overhanging trees,
I can taste the burning petrol,
I feel my hands blistering on the grips,
the muscles in my arms and shoulders
are pumping, hanging on,
my neck thickens under pressure
from the air trying to rip
the lid clean off my head,
I can hear the machine straining
towards maximum performance.
All sounds become a numbing blur
like on a plane descending sharply
from a great height; yet it's my ears
that take over from my eyes
as a sense of balance assumes control.
My perception is on a roll:
when I'm leaning the bike over
to the point where my kneepads kiss
the road surface, it feels as though I'm
perfectly in tune with the earth's axis.

Up and over Ago's Leap,
bit of a front wheel wobble
as she touches down,
sharp right hand at Quarter Bridge,
second gear, Bradden Bridge,
accelerate out with another wheelie,
Glen Loch, Glen Vine, flat out
for two and a half miles into Crosby,
through the corner, past the hotel

and instantly fall under the spell
of some tasty bird with a pint of best.
I met my first big love
on the shop floor at the local brewery,
we were 16 and I just knew
that Kirsty was the one for me.
I made a straight line for her,
asked her for a date,
told her she had to go out with me,
I was going to make her rich and famous
'cause one day I'd be a champion rider.
It didn't last,
she said two wheels have no class
and gave me up for a flash car.
Can't see what Kirsty saw in him,
he was all rear spoilers and walnut dash.
Still, you never forget your first, do you?
There'll always be a pillion seat
for Kirsty in my heart.

I keep seeing flashes
of another rider up ahead
but there can't be?
I was first out and no one's passed me.
Am I seeing things?
It's definitely a production machine
going very fast, but there are no markings,
no black reg plate issued for this race,
no official team colours or badge,
I can't quite see his number properly,
I don't even recognise the rider's style.
If only I could catch him.

Flat out on Sulby Straight,
180 m.p.h.,
then brake on the approach to Sulby Bridge,
down to 50-60 or I won't make it.
I've made that mistake before:
the first time I ever tackled this course
I ended up in that field,
I couldn't brake in time and ploughed
through the right-turn arrows,
I hit the giant billboard
doing about 100,
smashed clean through it
and skidded into the mud.
I was so relieved to be covered in cowshit,
I tell you, it's not how fast you're going
that matters, it's what you hit.

My best mate, Jock, wasn't so lucky:
lost it on Ramsay Hairpin, gears locked,
mechanical fault, nothing he could do,
bike smashed into a black commentary box
in front of a stone wall. The race was stopped
as the helicopter flew him to hospital.
He was dead on arrival.
Jock had a camera
fixed to his bike at the time,
he knew he was about to die.
I have heard his split-second scream,
his final breath,
over and over again.
Rewind, fast forward, pause,

the outcome is always the same,
he filmed his own death.
His wife brought his ashes back to the island,
she rode pillion with me
to the site of the crash.
We took Jock for one final journey,
scattering his ashes along
every twist and turn.
I wonder if they'll do the same for me?
Ashes to ashes,
crash to crashes,
that's how we live,
that's how we die.
It could be on a racetrack
or fetching fish and chips,
it's live to ride,
ride to live.

Every second counts climbing out
of the Hairpin, leaving loneliness
behind, through Gooseneck, I love this bit,
past No. 26, Joey's milestone
with his famous yellow helmet,
past the Guthrie memorial,
building up speed for the mountain mile,
make a mental note of the marshal's flag,
keep an eye out for sudden fog,
lying deep in the seat,
a quick meander through the Verandah,
taking four bends in one sweep,
picking it up, dropping it down,

picking it up, dropping it down
into a left-hander
and the 30 mile mark,
7 ¾ miles to go,
Bungalow Bridge, past the museum,
chasing my own tail over the railway
and into Windy Corner,
easy does it, respect the weather,
at this point the wind can choose to blow
a rider clean off the road,
flat out downhill towards homebase,
33rd milestone,
another blind bend, staring into space,
must have the confidence and courage
to take on the emptiness,
power over the rise to Kate's Cottage,
straighten the handlebars,
take off on the bump, gliding along,
then kill it to 50 at Creg-Ny-Baa,
power on full,
190 m.p.h
towards *the Cutting*.

It's not really a cutting at all,
but at that speed your perspective alters,
the road looks narrower
than it really is. In the patchy fog
up ahead, I catch another glimpse
of the rider, a fleeting shadow
dressed in black leathers and a grey lid,
gloves like claws instead of hands,

huge arms bending out at the elbow,
creating an enormous wingspan.
There is a supernatural roar
from his machine as he disappears
into the eye of the cutting.
There's no way I'll ever catch him.

Through Hillberry and Cronk-ny-Mona,
slow right at Signpost Corner,
mini-roundabout, bottom gear
through Governor's Bridge,
leaving nothing to chance, steer
carefully so as not to overbalance.
This is the slowest part of the race
so lots of keen photographers
jostling for the best place to distract you.
The irony is that riding this slow
can be as tricky as going fast.
It's like coming out of a trance
dropping from 190
to under 30 in such a short distance,
it's very easy to fall off
which makes for an embarrassing photograph.

Bombing it down Glencrutchery Road
and into gasoline alley
for the first and last pit-stop.
Halt at the gate, then accelerate
into a shock of mechanics.
It's the end of a mean lap one, two to go.
I'm still in the lead; how can that be?

No sign of the phantom rider.
I want to ask the team if they've seen him?
In the TT you're racing against yourself,
the only thing anyone notices is the clock.
Everything happens so quickly
in the pits, it's a shock to the system:
over the shoulder of one mechanic
hangs an industrial fuel pipe
like a giant viper about to strike,
a key opens my petrol tank,
fuel is delivered under pressure
at great speed from drip-feed pumps
while another tube is fed
through my lid, between my lips and into
my mouth, to upstream an energy drink,
a marshal conducts routine safety checks
and all of us are thinking
how to make the most of every second,
tyres are swopped: wets for drys
in response to the change in weather,
the new tyres are as smooth as a rubber
at the end of a pencil,
someone replaces my visor
and cleans my windshield with a chamois;
a proper pit-stop is a perfect cameo
of time hijacked by teamwork.
I miss the human contact
when I'm out there, alone on the track,
it's a solitary business being
the one at the centre of all this.

Lap two is about keeping it going,
clocking up, as near as damn it,
two miles every minute.
I have to win this race.
I always try and ride
in my No. 8 colours;
but there was some mix-up today
and no one could find them in the pits.
I kicked up a stink when they said
it's only superstition;
if they think I'm playing at this,
they're mighty wrong, I'm on a mission, me.
It's more than a lucky number,
I was born on the $8^{th}$ day of the $8^{th}$ month,
I met my wife, Katy, on the $8^{th}$.
How could she leave me?
I'm a successful rider,
I'll be a champion one day.

I'm flying through Kirk Michael village
at 90 m.p.h.
in what's normally a 30 zone,
past the schoolhouse and Mitre Hotel.
I love it when all the posh hotels
are full of leathers and jeans,
where bikers are treated like kings and queens.
I took Katy once to a restaurant
in Castleton, Derbyshire, nothing fancy,
two houses knocked into one.
We hung our helmets and found a table,
as a waitress was taking our order

the manager told us they weren't able
to serve us – they were closing early,
they'd run out of food, the chef
was in a bad mood, every excuse
under the sun. My wife said,
we're obviously spoiling
your up-market image and suggested
we leave, which made my blood boil.
Up-market, I said to him, up-yours!
I spread-eagled myself like a giant bird,
released a vicious cry
and, in one fell swoop,
trashed the table and chairs
with my leather and steel boots.
It wasn't enough to wreck the nest,
I had to regulate its keeper.
Katy pleaded with me to leave
as I took the manager by the throat
and made him apologise to my wife.
I didn't care if she found this ruthless
side of me unbearably ugly;
as far as I'm concerned it's not winning
that's uncouth, but losing.

Out of Kirk Michael village
towards Rhencullen, keep it vertical
over the bump, I'll be in trouble
if it's leaning when I land,
then on to the hump-back bridge at Ballaugh,
taking off with complete abandon –
try doing that in a car.

I love the place-names here
on this ancient outcrop
between Britain and Ireland,
rising up from the sea
to assert its independence
despite its common ancestry.
I share a similar psyche:
I have to be in charge of my own destiny,
I could never ride pillion with anyone.
My mum prefers to be a passenger
and, if she can, she'll walk;
she says she used to walk everywhere
as a girl, back home in County Cork.
When I was little she owned a car,
as a single mum it was her lifeline;
we were a team, me and my mum,
we had some great times.
It was my uncle Russ introduced me
to the buzz of biking.
He took me out dozens of times
on his classic 250 Matchless,
searching for reservoirs,
it was like a quest,
we were two-wheel explorers
on the green and grey hills of Derbyshire,
Yorkshire and Lancashire.
At each res we'd stop for a rest,
he'd get out his map and draw
a line to the next one;
he'd say, you can't beat hills and water
for a proper bike ride. He was right,

that's why I love it here on the island,
I never feel the cold and the wet,
besides you soon forget about it.
Russ wasn't really my uncle
but he was the best man I ever met;
he's not with us now, there's only my mum left.
My favourite place was Ladybower
'cause we could follow a road
all the way around the reservoirs;
sometimes the water would be flowing
over the damn walls, other times
it was bone dry if there'd been no rainfall.
Whenever I asked him about my dad
he'd say there was nothing to tell.
Dad went back to Dundee where
he was from; apparently;
he had another family up there.
For years I couldn't understand
how any man could lose touch
with his own children, seems a bit much,
unnatural even, until
you suffer such a thing yourself.
One Christmas morning,
I took Katy to Ladybower:
the res was virtually empty,
we could see the sunken village
rising above the water line;
we walked across the water
on the rooftops of the ruins
like a couple of miracle workers
out for a mid-day stroll.

She wore a full-length cloak
with shiny red lining,
as graceful as a redwing,
her dark hair spilled over the collar,
down her back and I loved her
more than words can say. That night
she conceived our first child, David.
Katy often came to see me race
but she wasn't really interested,
it wasn't her place in life.
I was away a lot from home,
I took on too much, I burned out,
my wife was alone with a young child,
my performance suffered,
I wanted to be with my family.
I turned down a few top offers,
suddenly my sponsor dropped me,
I panicked, became hell to live with;
we fell on hard times: no money,
another baby, Michelle, on the way,
I sold my own personal bike
to buy things for the baby,
I swore I'd give up racing for Katy
if that's what it took for us to stay
together; but she left me anyway.

I return to an empty nest
to find my mate and chicks have flown,
I fly around in a circle, frantically
searching every tree, bush, stone.
There must be some mistake:

it's the wrong nest,
they've nipped out for supper,
it's some sort of test.
I inspect the nest again for clues
but nothing has changed since
I left earlier in the day
to go out hunting for food.
I fly to higher ground:
I can see nothing.
I fall silent and listen
but I cannot hear them calling.
Palpatations, my body is racing
towards a heart-attack, my mind
is racing towards a panic-attack,
I am flying straight at a brick wall,
I scream inside my helmet
where no one can hear me,
where no one can witness my pain,
I screech at the north wind,
and call out their names.

This is where I had my worst breakdown,
at Parliament Square in Ramsay
which is just above sea-level
and the lowest point on the island.
First race of the season,
I was in the lead,
my entire career at stake
when the engine cut-out, died,
couldn't make it fire again;
such a public place to end the ride,

it hurt my pride more than anything,
no physical injuries this time
yet I was like a bird with a broken wing:
how could I ever fly again?
She took our baby daughter and son,
I took to the bottle, drugs,
any trick I could lay my hands on.
I was in a bedsit, licking
my wounds, smashing
up furniture, carving
love-letters into the brickwork, fighting
in the street, running
from the police, learning
the hard way, the way most of us learn
that, ultimately, I am alone on planet Earth.
On Mad Sunday,
the circuit is open to anyone
wishing to put their bravery
and skill to the test and, yes,
sometimes to the death;
but ride along Snake Pass,
the Cat and Fiddle or take any
of the great motorcycling roads
around the UK and you will witness
by the roadside the bouquets of flowers
and photos of loved ones,
marking their final moments.
People who don't ride
always feel
the need to tell you an apocryphal
motorcycle story, usually

related second or third hand
from a Casualty Nurse
about the rider who lost his head
in a head-on collision with a low-loader.
Bikers, on the other hand, will tell you
about their mate, Midas, down the Spread Eagle
who lost his leg and still rides,
using his good leg like a sidestand
or their mate, Spike, who's built himself
a left-handed trike rather than
give up riding altogether.
When Mad Sunday comes 'round again,
these are the kind of people who are there
to experience the zen of motorcycling.

My Mad Sunday lasted three years.
All I cared about was the next
Miss Wet T-Shirt Competition,
throwing banknotes at teenage lapdancers,
bungee jumping off the prom
and yards of Bushy's Ale or Okells Bitter.
I collected tattoos and piercings
like I used to collect press-cuttings –
no problem identifying
my corpse when the time comes.

On to the mountain mile,
looking for markers, trying
to find my bearings on the white lines
flashing in and out of view.
You'd think it would be easier downhill,

but it's much harder than going uphill:
it's harder to slow down once
you're accelerating out of control,
there is no speedo and no real need
of a rev counter, if you know
the sound of your own engine.
This bike is very forgiving:
I can push it to the limit,
I can punish it and it will
still perform to its best.
It's not simply a desire to win,
there is also a fear of losing:
I have battled against cynicism,
I refuse to be bitter,
Katy has gone, that's the end of it.
She gave me a son and a daughter
which is something to thank her for,
she was always straight with me,
there was a time Katy loved me
and that is something to celebrate;
now she is my ex,
time to move on to the next lap.
Tomorrow I will go and see my kids
and take them under my wing,
I'll teach our fledglings everything I know
and share with them the secrets of flying.

It is such a great feeling,
tear-arsing past the grandstand
at 170 m.p.h.
while still changing up to top gear.

I glance across at the podium
and imagine myself perched
on the top step
in the winner's red cap,
king of all the birds,
a laurel around my neck,
a handshake from a racing legend,
a kiss from a famous model
and a shower of champagne
in a slow-motion moment of bliss.
I have worn the green and blue caps before,
I am one single lap away from wearing the red.

I announce my comeback along Peel Road,
screeching like a banshee past the Highlander,
Greeba Castle and Cronk Dhoo Farm;
at Greeba Bridge they know I'm here,
powering through the left-right chicane
at Black Dub, caning it past Sarah's Cottage
on to the Cronk-y-Voddy
and the blind double 'S' bend at Handley's.
This is the courage corner
where races are won and lost:
who can take a corner like this on trust?
Who has enough faith in their ability
to push themselves to the limit?
I stare into nothingness
and create my own being,
making it up as I go along.
How much do I want to be a champion?
In this void I am chasing my own shadow,

the grey and black phantom rider,
the Crow
who straightens corners,
who finds the shortest line
and flies the quickest time.
I am determined to keep pace with him,
I can win this race.
I look out at the fields
and smell the freshly-cut grass,
I will not live in the past,
I will not live forever,
I am alive, this is what matters.

I am neck and neck with the Crow
as we fly down Glencrutchery Road
towards the finish line. It clicks
that he is wearing my lucky No. 8.
Time and place are playing tricks
inside the outer spaces
of my mind. I see them all,
lined up alongside the racetrack:
my friends, enemies, lovers, family,
the dad I never knew,
my best mate Jock,
my mum I owe everything to,
my compassionate uncle Russ,
Kirsty my first love,
my ex-wife Katy
with our son David and daughter Michelle;
I see them all in a split-second,
in the waving of a flag,

a photo-finish
between me and the Crow.
I double back in a figure of eight
into the winners' enclosure
and demand to see the time-lapse photo.
The marshals don't seem to know
what my problem is and gladly show me
a computer print of the finish.
I see myself looking directly
at the sun. I don't know how, but
I am wearing my lucky
No. 8 colours, after all.
There is no Crow, only me
and a faint grey and black shadow.
I have won.
I am a champion.

# Motorcycling

*You'll be doing 180mph and the bike lifts up on the back wheel and it's just a mega feeling...It's not just me job, it's me life. Everything I do is bike related. I love anything to do with bikes.* **David Jefferies**

*One of god's greatest challenges is to race a motorcycle, it's as simple as that... To go down Bray Hill on a bike is better than having sex.* **Bill Smith**

*There's a gyroscopic feel about a motorcycle that is extraordinary. You're taken onto a different plain 'cause the concentration level is heightened; everything, all your reactions are absolutely on the edge. You're right at the limit of what humans can withstand, I suppose.*
**Nick Jefferies**

*It's very addictive racing a motorcycle. I can't describe it any better than that.* **Jack Wood**

# The TT

*In 1907 when they thought about the first TT, the Tourist Trophy, in those days they set off with spares on their bikes and cloth caps and no leathers. In many ways, there's still the same spirit of setting off on a long journey. When you go to ride six laps around here, it's 226 miles and it's basically an ordinary road.*
**Nick Jefferies**

*The TT is a festival on its own. The circuit is something that is very special, very different to anywhere else in the world. The buzz you get from riding around the circuit on ordinary roads. I've always liked to go fast, getting from A to B quick has always been a challenge as far as I'm concerned.* **Tony Jefferies**

*The thing with the Isle of Man is, it's the buzz you get, you can't replicate anywhere else, there's no other race like it, it's just you against the circuit.* **David Jefferies**

# The Danger

*I came back to racing three years after the accident 'cause I still enjoyed doing it. If you enjoy doing something why should you give it up?*

*When they said to me, we can only fix your arms in one position, I thought, well, I'll have them fixed for riding a bike. So I did race again afterwards. If it had to be locked in one position, might as well get it in the position it suits you. I mean, I can ride a bike and everything else, I have trouble wiping my backside, but that's besides the point.*
**Bill Smith**


*All I've ever known is motorbikes so racing's where all my friends are and where my life's always been. It would have been difficult to say I'm not going back again to the TT after Steve died... I mean, life's dangerous. If you backed away from everything where people got hurt or killed, you wouldn't be moving out of your own house. So, no, you've got to live life.* **Yvonne Ward**


Since the BBC Radio 4 broadcast of "Racer", which included these interviews, TT World Champion David Jefferies died, tragically, in practice on his beloved Isle of Man circuit.

# Credits

*Racer was commissioned by BBC Radio 4 Drama*
*and broadcast on 9th December, 2002*
*Directed and produced by Nadia Molinari*
*Performed by Paul McGann*
*Interviews by Clare Jenkins*
*Sound Design & Edit by Eloise Whitmore*
*Additional Editing by Steve Brooke*

**Special thanks** to Tony Jefferies, Nick Jefferies, Irene Thomas, Bill Smith, Yvonne Ward, Des & Wyn Evans, Jack Woods, Robin Jameson, Geoff Duke and the late David Jefferies.

Thanks also to Stephen Feber, Melanie Harris, Ross Bradshaw, Darren Poyzer, Helen Riley

**Cover illustration**: Clifford Harper

# Kevin Fegan

Playwright & Poet, Kevin Fegan has written over thirty plays for the stage, several plays for BBC Radio 4 Drama (including a Woman's Hour Serial and a Classic Serial), two short films, several volumes of poetry plus a spell as a Storyline Writer for Coronation St. Kevin is a regular performer of his own poetry at live readings and on national radio and television.

Kevin is co-founder of Lonesome Trail Pictures and Big Theatre Company.

For more information about Kevin's work, please visit his website: www.kevinfegan.co.uk

Kevin's epic dramatic poems, *Blast* and *Let Your Left Hand Sing* are also published by Five Leaves.

# Also from Kevin Fegan by Five Leaves

*"Life is a good fire
around which stories are told
and, in the end, when the fire goes out,
all we are left with are words."*

Kevin Fegan explores the poetry to be found in heavy industry — and it doesn't come much heavier than steel. *Blast* is the fictional tale of a retired steelworker from the Templeborough melting shop in South Yorkshire. After 40 years of dirt and graft, laughter and sweat, he is determined to enjoy his early retirement, even if it kills him.

"Kevin Fegan is a poet and a playwright with a capacity for sympathetic identification and a taste for tough, complex issues." THE GUARDIAN

"Fegan runs ever faster to keep his work at the leading edge of contemporary life" THE INDEPENDENT

"Britain's most innovative playwright" PLAYS INTERNATIONAL

## Blast was first broadcast on Radio 4

A6, 48 pages, 0907123392, £4.50